smart girl's GUIDE™

TRAVEL

everything you need to know
about adventuring near and far

by Aubre Andrus
illustrated by Stevie Lewis

Published by American Girl Publishing

No part of this book may be used or reproduced in any manner whatsoever without written permission except in the case of brief quotations embodied in critical articles and reviews.

19 20 21 22 23 24 25 QP 10 9 8 7 6 5 4 3 2 1

Editorial Development: Barbara E. Stretchberry
Art Direction and Design: Jessica Rogers
Illustrations: Stevie Lewis
Production: Jessica Bernard, Caryl Boyer, Kristi Lively, Cynthia Stiles

For Mira
—Aubre Andrus, author

Library of Congress Cataloging-in-Publication Data

Names: Andrus, Aubre, author. | Lewis, Stevie, illustrator.
Title: A smart girl's guide, travel : everything you need to know about adventuring near and far / by Aubre Andrus ; illustrated by Stevie Lewis.
Description: Middleton, WI : American Girl Publishing, 2019.
Identifiers: LCCN 2018002862 | ISBN 9781683371236
Subjects: LCSH: Travel—Juvenile literature.
Classification: LCC G175 .A56 2019 | DDC 910.835/2—dc23
LC record available at https://lccn.loc.gov/2018002862

americangirl.com/service

Dear Reader,

Travel is about exploration and adventure. It's about trying new things and meeting new people. Sounds fun—and maybe a little bit scary—right? But when you take on a challenge, you learn a lot. And there's so much out there to discover.

Imagine yourself right now in your neighborhood. Now zoom out and imagine your hometown, then your state, then the entire country, and, finally, the whole planet. You are one tiny pixel in a much bigger picture. It's pretty exciting when you think about it. Earth is made up of seven continents and 195 countries. The world is filled with interesting people (over 7 billion of them!), incredible sights, cool animals, and amazing food.

This book shows you how to be a safe and happy traveler, whether you are going to your grandma's house just a few hours away or you're making a trek across the world. There's so much to see! Why not start exploring right now in your own backyard?

Happy travels,

Your friends at American Girl

contents

WHY DO WE TRAVEL? ✈

TAJ MAHAL

To see history come to life

To experience a culture different from our own

To meet people we've only read or heard about

CLEOPATRA

To try new foods

TIRAMISU

To do something that might seem scary—but ends up being fun

To learn what we have in common

NIAGARA FALLS

To see beautiful places and famous sights

To learn about ourselves and others

travel dreams

Creating a list of dream destinations is a fun way to record your experiences and keep track of what you want to see. Your list can be as big or as small as you'd like, and you can always add to it. Remember, you have your whole life ahead of you!

Here are some ideas to get you started:

- Visit all fifty states
- Walk on seven continents
- Road-trip from the East Coast to the West Coast
- Identify every country on a map
- Ride a train across Europe
- Live in a foreign country
- See penguins in the wild
- Visit every baseball stadium in the United States
- See the New Seven Wonders of the World
- Take in the view from the world's tallest buildings
- Camp in all 59 U.S. national parks
- Photograph every waterfall in your state

- See the ten most famous paintings in person
- Swim in all five of the world's oceans
- Travel to 100 countries
- Go scuba diving
- Hike some of the tallest mountains in the world
- Learn another language
- Visit your state's capitol building
- See a lion, elephant, buffalo, leopard, and rhinoceros on an African safari
- Explore your city— on your bike!
- Visit the moon (Hey, it could happen!)

Display your travel dreams

Instead of a list, create a piece of art to display in your room that will inspire your *wanderlust*, or thirst for adventure.

ADVENTURE AWAITS!

Vision board

Create a vision board with photos of all the places you'd like to travel to one day. Find images online and print them. Glue them onto a poster or pin them to a bulletin board.

World map

Attach a map of the world or the United States to a bulletin board. Use two different colors of thumb-tacks to pin the places you have visited as well as the places you'd like to visit.

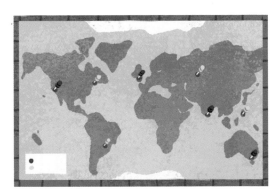

How to visit imaginary places

Your favorite books, movies, and TV shows were probably inspired by real places that you can actually visit today. For example, there are a lot of cool wizard-themed filming locations in the United Kingdom and lots of fun filming sites in Los Angeles and New York. To find them, search online for "filming locations" and the name of your fave movie or TV show.

9

how adventurous are you?

When it comes to the unknown, do you test the waters or dive right in?

1. Your friend got a new video game for her birthday and she invites you over to play. You've never played before so you . . .

   a. ask her what the game is like.

   b. say yes right away.

   c. see if she'd be willing to play something you know instead.

2. You're standing in front of a big pool and you know the water will be cold. You . . .

   a. wait for a friend to jump in first and tell you how freezing it feels.

   b. are the first to take the plunge!

   c. slowly wade into the pool by taking the stairs.

CANNON BALL!

3. You're at a friend's house for dinner and her parents serve you something you've never seen before. You . . .

   a. ask what it is and what it's made from.

   b. take a few bites. Who knows? You might like it.

   c. politely say, "No, thank you."

4. Something you would never do is . . .

   a. scuba diving, but you would try snorkeling.

   b. you don't know— you'll try anything once!

   c. skydiving. It looks terrifying!

5. Your parents signed you up for a sleepaway camp this summer and you won't know anyone. You . . .

   a. totally freak out but once you learn more about it, you start to get excited.

   b. are looking forward to making some new friends.

   c. beg your friends to sign up too so you won't have to go alone.

6. Your best friend speaks Spanish at home. You . . .

a. ask her to teach you a few words.

b. surprise her by learning how to say, "You're awesome!"

c. are amazed because learning another language sounds really hard.

7. A new kid in your class has lived all over the world because his mom was in the military. You . . .

a. like to hear stories about what his other schools were like.

b. have a million questions for him—what a cool experience!

c. can't even imagine moving around so much. No thanks!

8. When you're an adult, you'd like to . . .

a. get an apartment in a big city.

b. study abroad in another country.

c. live in the same neighborhood where you grew up.

Answers

If you picked **mostly a's,** you're open to adventure. You are thoughtful and a good researcher. Before diving into something new, you want to know exactly what you're getting into. It makes you feel more comfortable. And that's not a bad thing. You know what you like and what you don't like, but you'll push your limits occasionally. When it comes to travel, a tour group might be perfect for you. A knowledgeable guide will show you the way so you can feel comfortable knowing you're in good hands.

If you picked **mostly b's,** you're a full-blown adventurer! You're brave and confident. You're not afraid to try new things or go to a place you've never been. You like to say yes! No matter how much you do or see, you are open to a new experience. You're OK with taking the lead and wandering off the beaten path. When it comes to travel, you'd enjoy planning a trip from start to finish on your own—leaving plenty of time to explore, of course. Remember to enjoy the current moment instead of getting too caught up in the next big adventure.

If you picked **mostly c's,** you're a beginner explorer. You're a little reluctant when it comes to trying new things. Your first reaction is usually no because you like to stay in your comfort zone—and that's OK. But every once in a while, it's good to dip your toe in the water. More often than not, you'll discover that something new is actually something you love. But you'll never know unless you try! Start small by visiting a museum, library, or park that you've never been to or tasting a food you've never tried before.

BE PREPARED

A fun part of travel is the prepping and planning beforehand.

Where will we go?

- LONDON
- TEL AVIV
- OSLO
- BANGKOK
- VANCOUVER
- CAIRO

What will we do?

What will I wear?

WHAT'S IN YOUR SUITCASE?

ROME, ITALY

NYCity

ICELAND

What bag
should I
bring?

PASSPORT

Do I need a
passport?

2-WAY RETURN TICKET

How will we
get there?

SEAT
13B

14:15

VALID NOW = ROUTE ANYWHERE

COLETTE INN
HOW CAN WE ASSIST YOU?

Where will
we stay?

LONDON
MAR 3
IMMIGRA

What will we eat?

make an itinerary

An itinerary is a list of what you want to do on your trip. As a family, you can gather ideas by researching on the Internet or checking out travel books from the library. Make a giant list of all the cool things you could do and then narrow it down. You don't want to overplan, or you'll end up exhausted and stressed out. Leave some time to just wander around. And make sure everyone in the family gets to see or do at least one thing that excites them.

LE MARCHÉ

Travel Tip: Research places to eat, too. When you're tired and hungry, it will be nice to have a few options already figured out.

If you're leaving the country

An international trip takes a little bit more preparation. In addition to creating an itinerary, your family might want to do some extra research to learn about the food, language, and weather.

If you're traveling to a country where the people speak another language, explore the language resources at the library or download a basic language app with your parent's permission. Learning how to say hello, good-bye, please, and thank you can be really helpful.

If you're concerned about the food, try the country's cuisine at a local restaurant so you'll get an idea of what you might like. No matter where you travel in the world, you can usually find unique sandwiches, noodle and rice dishes, soups, and pastries.

Do you need a passport?

If you're flying outside the United States, you'll need a passport. Even babies need passports! A passport is an official document with your photo and personal information. It allows the government to protect you while you travel to another country.

Wondering why your passport is a booklet with blank pages? It's for stamps. Each time you visit another country, you'll get a new stamp when you enter and sometimes when you leave. The stamp usually includes the date, and it means that you have been approved to visit the country for a certain amount of time.

how to pack

Packing is a skill that you'll get better at with practice. Start thinking about what you need a week before you leave.

Don't overpack

Packing light means you'll only bring the essentials. When you pack light, you can carry your own stuff, keep track of it, and easily unpack and repack it. Think about what you will actually want to wear and use each day.

What do you need for a seven-day trip?

- 7 pairs of underwear (and socks if needed)

- 2 pairs of shoes (so you can alternate if your feet hurt)

- 2–3 bottoms such as pants, shorts, or skirts

- 5–7 tops such as tank tops or T-shirts

- A jacket, sweater, or scarf to keep you warm on the plane or at night

- 1–2 sets of pajamas

- A reuseable bag (for dirty clothes, souvenirs, or to use as a day bag)

- Optional: a swimsuit, snow pants, a fancy dress, or whatever else you'll need that's specific to your trip

Travel Tip: If you aren't positive that you'll use something during your trip, don't bring it "just in case." You can usually buy it once you get there if you really need it.

Travel Tip: Check the weather forecast for your destination before you pack.

17

get coordinated

Pack complete outfits that already match and are ready to wear. In fact, pack some of your favorite outfits that fit well and make you feel great. (Packing a brand-new outfit isn't a good idea. What if it ends up being uncomfortable?) If you pack clothing and accessories that are in the same color family, you can easily mix and match them during your trip to create even more outfits.

7 pieces of clothing, 6 different outfits

Travel Tip:

Layering with a cardigan or scarf can help you create even more outfits when matched with different tops. A scarf can double as a light blanket, too.

Don't forget the toiletries

You'll need toothpaste and a toothbrush, plus a hairbrush or comb and a few of your favorite hair accessories. Most hotels have soap, shampoo, conditioner, lotion, and a hair dryer. Put all toiletries in plastic zip-top bags so they don't leak.

Something extra

When you travel, you won't have a lot of the comforts from your home. But a small pillow, nightlight, or stuffed animal may make you feel a little more comfortable and help you sleep better.

Fold or roll?

Some travelers swear that rolling clothes instead of folding them saves room in your suitcase and makes clothing less wrinkly. Try both ways and see what you think. Here's another tip worth trying: Packing cubes are zippered compartments that can help keep your clothing organized and keep clean and dirty clothes separate during your trip.

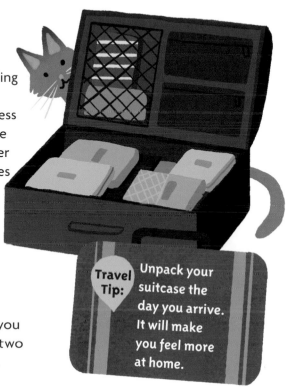

Travel Tip: Unpack your suitcase the day you arrive. It will make you feel more at home.

Luggage lingo

If you're flying somewhere, you have the option of bringing two types of bags to the airport.

Carry-on

A carry-on bag is small enough to fit underneath the airplane seat in front of you or above your seat in the overhead compartment. Carry-on bags are perfect for snacks, a book, and headphones. You'll have to carry this bag around the airport and through the security lines so make sure it's not too heavy, and make sure it zips or buckles on top so things don't fall out.

Checked bag

A checked bag is a larger piece of luggage that's given to the airline when you first check in at the airport. The airline makes sure your bag gets onto the correct plane. Checked bags are stored in the cargo compartment in the bottom of the plane during the flight. When you arrive, the bags are brought to the baggage claim area, where passengers pick them up. Most people pack their clothes, shoes, and toiletries in checked bags.

GETTING THERE

How you travel to your destination is part of the fun.

Look up! At any moment, there are about 10,000 planes in the air.

PATAGONIA
APR 2 2010

Route 66 is a famous highway that travels through eight states from Chicago, Illinois, to Santa Monica, California. It's a favorite road trip for many families!

JUNEAU
04 JUL 1[?]
ALAS[?]

Some cruise ships travel around the entire world! It takes more than 100 days to complete the trip.

It takes 51 hours—one way—for the California Zephyr to travel from Chicago to San Francisco.

SINGLE PASSENGER

NYC → BOS

You can take a bus up and down the East Coast and see cities such as Charleston, Philadelphia, and Boston along the way.

BUS TICKET

It would take 40 hours to drive nonstop from Washington, D.C., to San Francisco.

03 SEPT 12

NORWAY

at the airport

Airports are busy, busy, busy! There are so many people coming and going, traveling near and traveling far. The airports in Atlanta, Chicago, and Los Angeles are among the busiest in the world.

You need to be extra cautious when you're at any airport. You have to keep track of your belongings, stay out of everyone's way, and follow the rules very carefully.

 1. Arrive early: two hours before your flight, or three hours early if you are leaving the country.

 2. Check in. Your family can do this online or at the counter at the airport. You'll get a boarding pass with a seat number.

 3. Check your large bags at the counter. Bring your carry-on bag with you.

 4. Go through the security checkpoint.

 5. Walk to your gate (check the big "departures" monitors if your gate number isn't listed on your boarding pass).

 6. Go to the bathroom, fill up your water bottle, and get some snacks. Now wait patiently to board the plane.

Flying is fun

Riding in an airplane is such a cool experience. You're super high up in the air and you're traveling super fast. The views are awesome! And once you land, you're in a totally new place. How amazing is that?

Some people do get a little nervous on planes. Planes make a lot of noises, and sometimes there are bumps in the air—just like there are when a car drives over a bumpy road. If you get scared on the plane, just remember that the pilots will do everything they can to keep you safe. It's actually safer to ride in a plane than it is to ride in a car.

To calm your nerves, try closing the window shade, listening to music, reading a book, doing a crossword puzzle, or watching a movie. Or close your eyes and slowly breathe in and out ten times. You'll be there before you know it.

Flying alone?

Kids between ages 5 and 15 can fly alone as "unaccompanied minors." An airline representative will make sure you never walk alone in the airport, and she or he won't leave your side until you meet your family member at your destination. Listen carefully to directions, hang on to your travel documents, and you'll be fine!

staying safe at the airport

Because airports are so busy and there are so many people coming and going, there are strict rules that have to be followed to keep everything moving smoothly. Imagine a school with no rules—it would be total chaos!

Some of the most important rules are about what you can and can't bring on a plane. There are different rules for carry-on bags and checked bags (the ones people pick up at the baggage claim area once their plane lands). With a parent, check the current rules online at tsa.gov.

The best way to make sure all passengers follow these rules is by having everyone walk through a security checkpoint. Your luggage will get screened and so will you! The process can be a little stressful, but it helps keep everyone safe.

Here's how it works: You'll place your bag and belongings on a conveyor belt so they can be scanned; then you'll walk through a scanner or metal detector. That's it! After moving through the screening, you grab your belongings and walk to your gate.

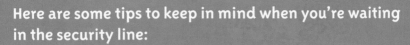

Here are some tips to keep in mind when you're waiting in the security line:

✈ Pay attention at all times.

✈ Follow all instructions.

✈ Be ready to quickly place your belongings on the conveyor belt.

✈ Wear shoes that are easy to slip off in case you need to remove them.

✈ Bring an empty water bottle to refill after you've passed though security.

✈ Pack solid snacks in your carry-on bag, not anything liquid.

Once you get through security, you can buy things like drinks, food, books, and more.

If you ever get separated from your family, walk up to any ticket counter or store register and ask the adult behind the desk to help you.

boredom busters

Whether you're in a bus, on a plane, on a train, or in a car, it's likely you'll have more than a few hours of time on your hands.

Conversation starters

Use this together time as a chance to really get to know your family. Write a list of questions that you can ask every member of your family. Some suggestions to get you started: What is your favorite food? What is your best memory? Where would you live if you could live anywhere in the world?

Who am I?

On scraps of paper or note cards, ask your family to write down famous people or characters. Collect the papers and mix them up. Now let one family member draw a name (but don't show it to anyone else). The other family members can ask yes-or-no questions to try to figure out who it is.

Scavenger hunt

Ask your family to help you create a list of items that you might see in the airport or on the road. Or try to find one item for each letter of the alphabet. See if you can cross everything off the list before you arrive at your destination.

Easy things to pack:

Notebook and colored pencils

Puzzle book

Magazine or book

Handheld video game

Coloring book

Card game

Music player and headphones

Journal and pen

Snacks for the road

Whenever you're traveling, it's good to have some snacks on hand. Travel plans don't always go perfectly, so it's possible that you could end up very hungry with no food in sight. Here are some snacks that are easy to travel with. Store them in zip-top bags.

Fresh fruit: grapes, strawberries, and orange slices

Trail mix: dry cereal, dried fruit, popcorn, pretzels, and chocolate pieces

Sandwich squares: cut a sandwich into quarters

Veggie mix: carrot sticks, cucumber slices, and cherry tomatoes

Cheese and crackers: string cheese or slices of cheese and whole-grain crackers

how should you get there?

There are so many cool ways to get where you want to go!

1. When it comes to traveling, you'd rather . . .

   a. get to your destination as quickly as possible.

   b. see the most interesting sights along the way.

   c. take the most comfortable way possible.

2. This weekend, you have to clean your room. You'd rather be told . . .

   a. to clean it at nine a.m. on Saturday.

   b. that it must be cleaned by Sunday night at nine p.m.

   c. a few different days and times when you could clean your room.

3. Your dream trip is . . .

   a. in another country.

   b. on the other side of the country.

   c. just an hour away.

4. When it comes to sleeping, you need . . .

   a. a comfortable bed and the lights off.

   b. only a comfy pillow.

   c. nothing. You can fall asleep anywhere.

5. If you were to travel a long distance, it would be most important to be able to . . .

   a. get up and walk around to stretch your legs.

   b. stop whenever you want to eat or use the bathroom.

   c. look out the window at a pretty view.

6. Your favorite part of traveling is . . .

   a. once you arrive!

   b. the time you get to spend with your family.

   c. the anticipation of getting there.

7. You'd love to . . .

   a. soar through the clouds.

   b. meander through big cities.

   c. zip-line through a forest.

Answers

If you picked **mostly a's,** you'll love a long plane ride. You have big plans to travel around the world, and the best way to do that is by plane. It's the fastest way to get somewhere. It might not be the most comfortable, but you'll be amazed how far you can go in such a short amount of time. Would you sit on a plane for ten hours if it meant you got to walk around Paris? *Mais oui!* (Of course!)

If you picked **mostly b's,** you'll love a good road trip. For destinations that are fairly close to your hometown, driving is the way to go. You can stop whenever you want for food or bathroom breaks, and you're bound to run into some cool sights on the way. Plus, you get to control the temperature and the radio station—with some help from your family, of course. That means you'll be pretty comfortable and get exactly where you need to go. Awesome!

If you picked **mostly c's,** you'll love an epic train ride. Traveling by train is great! No one has to drive, so your whole family gets to enjoy the views out the window, take a nap whenever they want, and walk around to stretch their legs. Train travel isn't always the fastest, but it is fun. Some trains even have sleeping compartments, bathrooms, and a dining car. Wow!

ADJUSTING

You've finally arrived! But you might have to deal with a few challenges before the fun can start.

Why am I so tired?

Where are we going first?

What time is it?

TAIP
12 JAN

travel trials

Sometimes when you travel, you're going to deal with a lot of people—both strangers and your own family. You may be in an unfamiliar place and you may have traveled very far, which means you could be tired and crabby once you get there. Travel isn't always easy!

Tight quarters

Staying in a hotel? You're probably not used to sharing a bedroom with your entire family—or sharing a bed with your sibling. But traveling usually requires getting cozy with others. Remember that it's a temporary situation, and that you'll spend very little time in your hotel room. It's just for sleeping! You'll be out exploring every day.

Group decisions

If you planned your trip as a family, you may have already experienced this challenge. Each family member will have a different idea of fun, so deciding what to do first will require cooperation. You're all traveling together, so you'll have to consider everyone's feelings.

Here are some tips to help with group decisions:

• Assign one day to each family member. That person gets to have the final say on that day's plans.

• Find a compromise: Maybe you can't eat pizza tonight but you can tomorrow.

• Take a family vote—majority wins. (If you have an even number, a parent gets to be the tiebreaker.)

i'm soooo tired!

Traveling can be tough on your body. Even though you're excited for your trip to start, you're probably exhausted. You might be dealing with less sleep, a different time zone, or way more walking than you are used to.

One way to fight the "I'm pooped!" feeling is to schedule a break every afternoon. Take a nap, read in bed, or rest in front of the TV. Be sure to drink a lot of water because it's easy to get dehydrated when you travel, which can give you headaches or make you feel constipated.

Plan B

No matter how perfectly your family plans a trip, something out of your control may alter those plans. That's just a part of traveling! A delayed flight, bad weather, or an early closing time can make you feel sad and upset. If you go into your trip knowing that everything won't be perfect, you'll be less likely to be disappointed when plans change.

You can't control everything that happens to you, but you can control your reaction. Stay positive, and get excited about a Plan B. Some of the best travel experiences happen when you have to turn left even though you wanted to turn right. Maybe seeking shelter from a sudden rainstorm leads you into an awesome art museum. Or a closed tourist attraction means you walk around the corner and find a delicious ice cream shop instead.

Travel Tip:

If you're traveling during a rainy week, keep your plans flexible so you can do the outdoor activities on the day it ends up being sunny.

time zones

What's the first thing people do when they arrive in a new place? Adjust their clocks. That's because when it's nine p.m. in New York City, it's nine a.m. *the next day* in Bangkok, Thailand. Huh? It's true—when kids in the United States are going to bed, Thai kids are eating breakfast.

The Earth is divided into twenty-four time zones. And every twenty-four hours, the Earth slowly turns one rotation. As the Earth rotates, it gets different amounts of sunlight, which create daytime and nighttime.

Time zones ensure that it's light during daytime hours and dark during nighttime hours no matter where you live. If there was only one time zone for the entire world, you might be eating lunch in complete darkness, at sunset, or during sunrise depending on where you lived.

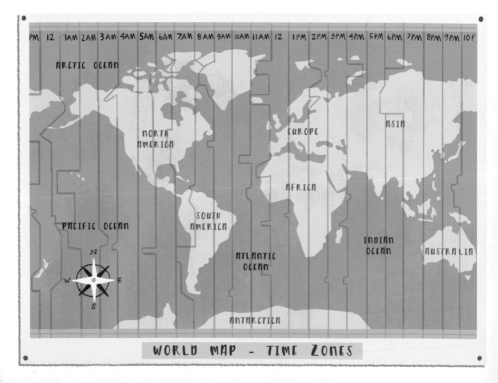

Jet lag

When you travel, you might be in a different time zone—it could be ahead of your regular time zone or behind it. The continental United States has four time zones: Pacific, Mountain, Central, and Eastern. Hawaii and Alaska are in two more time zones.

Let's say you live in South Carolina and you're flying to California. That's three time zones away, so it's a three-hour difference. When you arrive in California, it's six p.m. But it's nine p.m. back home, so your body might feel ready for bed even though the clock says it's time for dinner. That's called jet lag! But you don't have to take an airplane to feel jet lag—you can feel it after taking a train or driving, too.

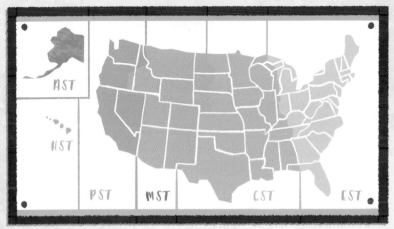

Jet lag usually is worse the farther you travel from home. If you travel from Boston to Rome, your plane might land at eight a.m. in Rome but it will feel like two a.m. to you. A six-hour time difference—yikes! You'll probably be tired during your first day in Italy.

It can take a couple of days to adjust to a time change. Here are some ways to help your body get over jet lag:

- Try to sleep on the plane—even a few hours can help.

- Adjust to the new time zone as quickly as possible. Try not to go to bed until your regular bedtime in the new time zone.

- Get outside. Sunlight can help you adjust to the new time zone more quickly.

- Drink a lot of water. Dehydration combined with a lack of sleep can make you feel sick.

- Don't calculate what time it is back at home. Thinking about it will probably make you feel more tired.

numbers game

Did you know that other parts of the world measure things differently than we do in the United States? Everything from time to temperature to shoe and clothing sizes to length and weight could be different. It might feel overwhelming at first, but you'll be surprised how quickly you can adjust to a new system.

Time

In the United States, we differentiate eight in the morning from eight at night by saying eight a.m. and eight p.m. Many other countries use a twenty-four-hour system to measure how long it's been since midnight. That means eight p.m. is 20:00.

How do you know what time it is? One a.m. to noon is the same. But from noon, you'll keep counting up (or just add twelve hours in your head). So one p.m. is 13:00, two p.m. is 14:00, and so on.

Instead of saying "thirteen o'clock," say "thirteen-hundred." To read 13:05, say "thirteen-oh-five." To tell the time between midnight and 12:59 a.m., it would be 0:00 to 0:59. So 0:30 would be "zero thirty."

Weather and distance

Even though we don't use it in the United States, the metric system is used in most other countries. Distances are measured in kilometers instead of miles, and temperature is measured in degrees Celsius instead of degrees Fahrenheit. So don't be alarmed if you read a speed limit sign or hear a weather report and think that something must be wacky. It's just the metric system!

32 degrees Fahrenheit = **0 degrees Celsius**

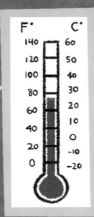

A beautiful 75-degree day is about 24 degrees Celsius.

1 mile = **1.6 kilometers**

If your parents are driving 35 miles per hour, they are driving about 56 kilometers per hour.

41

Currency conversion

Time and distance aren't the only things you'll have to convert when you are in another country. The currency, or money, will be different, too. You'll see all different kinds of colorful bills and cool coins. Some are so pretty that you'll want to keep them.

There are two things you need to think about when converting currency:

1. What kind of money does this country use?

2. What is its value?

For example, Sweden doesn't use the dollar; it uses the krona. Let's say that one U.S. dollar equals eight Swedish kronor. That means that a soda that costs two dollars in the United States would cost sixteen kronor in Sweden. So even though it sounds more expensive, it's the same amount.

16 kronor divided by 8 kronor = 2 U.S. dollars

The value of currency is different in every country. Things might not always be cheaper in other countries—they could be more expensive. For example, if you were traveling to London, you might learn that one British pound, the currency in the United Kingdom, is equivalent to about $1.31 in the United States. That means things in London might seem to cost more than what you are used to.

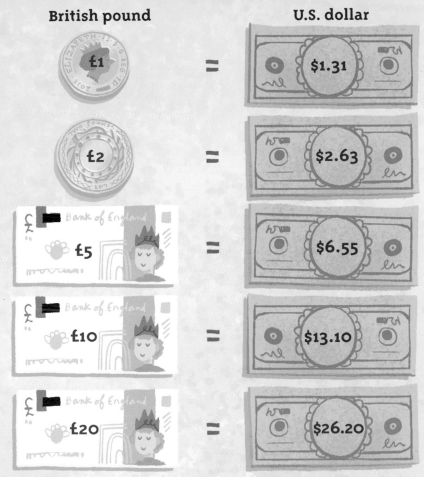

British pound		U.S. dollar
£1	=	$1.31
£2	=	$2.63
£5	=	$6.55
£10	=	$13.10
£20	=	$26.20

To better understand the value of money, your family can look up exchange rates online. The value of money changes a little bit every day. Sometimes the dollar is stronger, or worth more, and sometimes it is weaker, or worth less.

Your family will be paying with the local currency during your trip, so write down the U.S. dollar equivalent of the most common bills and coins of that country. Carry this cheat sheet with you so you have a better idea of what something costs when you want to purchase a souvenir or a snack.

Travel Tip:

Bring a little coin purse when traveling to another country. Many countries use coins more than we do, and some of those coins are worth as much as $1, $2, or even $5.

DEALING WITH DIFFERENCES

It's definitely not home, but that's exactly
what's so exciting about it.

China is one of many
Asian countries where
people eat with chop-
sticks instead of a fork.
Chopsticks are a pair
of smooth sticks held
between the thumb
and forefinger.

In Spain, a lot of people
take a *siesta*, which is
a nap or a long lunch
break, for a few hours
in the afternoon. Then
they eat a small dinner
at nine p.m. or later.

In places like Istanbul,
Turkey, some women
choose to wear a hijab,
which is a scarf that
covers their head and
hair, or a jilbab, which
covers their entire body
like a long, loose dress,
for religious reasons.

17 FEB 17
FRANCE

In the United Kingdom, people drive on the left side of the road instead of the right. That means you have to first look right when you cross the street.

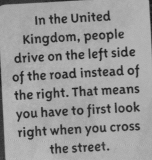

In Japan, some people sleep on *tatami*, which are thin mats that lay directly on the floor.

GENEVA
MAY 16
SWITZERLAND

In Ethiopia, food is eaten with one's hands. *Injera,* a spongy flat bread, is torn into pieces and used to scoop up meat and vegetables.

In some countries, you have to pay to use a public toilet. And in Asia, you may not have a seat but have to squat instead.

i'm not used to this!

The place you're traveling to is, well, not like home. But that's what makes traveling so interesting. You get to imagine what your life would be like if you lived in another part of the state, the country, or the world.

Be respectful

Just because something is different doesn't mean that it's weird, funny, or wrong. When you're walking around an unfamiliar place, make observations or even write notes in a travel journal. When you're back in a private place, like your hotel room, you and your family can talk about all the unique things you've seen. An adult can answer any questions you have, or you and your parents can research your questions on the Internet.

Keep these tips in mind when you travel to a new place:

⊘ Don't point.

⊘ Don't stare or make a surprised face.

⊘ Don't whisper mean things.

⊘ Don't take photos of strangers unless you ask permission.

How to dress

Different regions often have different ideas and expectations of what is considered the proper way to dress. In Asia or the Middle East, for example, women and girls often have to cover their shoulders and knees, so it's expected that visitors will, too—especially if you're visiting a temple or mosque. You may have to cover your head with a scarf and remove your shoes, too. If you're visiting a church in Europe, you might have to cover your shoulders with a scarf or sweater while you're inside.

These rules might mean that you can't wear shorts or tank tops even in the summer. If you're not sure what to wear, a tunic with leggings can be worn at any time of year and is a comfortable travel outfit. A cardigan or scarf can easily be carried along during a day of sight-seeing just in case you need to cover your shoulders.

The universal language

Be kind! No matter where you are in the world, kindness always makes a great first impression. If you're visiting a country where English is not spoken, try learning a few key phrases such as hello, good-bye, please, and thank you.

Even when you're traveling in the United States, you might learn some new phrases:

In the South, you'll hear "y'all" instead of "you guys."

Are your summer nights lit up with lightning bugs or fireflies? In the West, you'll almost always hear firefly.

In Wisconsin, they say "bubbler" instead of "water fountain."

Tennis shoes or sneakers? Usually only people on the East Coast say "sneakers."

Do you wear pa-jahh-mas or pa-jam-as? In the South and on the East Coast, people tend to say "ahh."

Travel Tip: To learn a few key phrases in another language, explore the language resources at your library or download a basic language app with your parents' permission.

how much do you know about the world?

See if you can answer these global trivia questions.

1. When you're in London, you'll use a WC. What is it?

   a. A bathroom

   b. A telephone

   c. A fork

2. In what country can you eat a hot soup with noodles and meat for breakfast?

   a. Chile

   b. Vietnam

   c. Sweden

3. How long is the longest nonstop flight in the world?

   a. 17 hours, 30 minutes

   b. 24 hours

   c. 9 hours, 45 minutes

4. The tallest building in the world is in what city?

　a. New York City, New York

　b. Tokyo, Japan

　c. Dubai, United Arab Emirates

5. In Australia, the summer season is . . .

　a. June to August.

　b. March to May.

　c. December to February.

6. In Fairbanks, Alaska, the longest day of summer is how long?

　a. 22 hours

　b. 18 hours

　c. 12 hours

7. Where can you see some of the smallest penguins in the world and some of the largest turtles in the world?

　a. Costa Rica

　b. Galapagos Islands

　c. The Great Barrier Reef

8. In the United States, the weather is warmer in the South. In South America, the weather is . . .

a. colder as you head south.

b. warmer as you head south.

c. the same as you head south.

9. In many Asian countries, you must do what before entering a home?

a. Take off your shoes

b. Introduce yourself

c. Knock three times

10. Where can you find the world's longest river?

a. Australia

b. Asia

c. Africa

Answers

1. a. WC stands for "water closet."

2. b. It's called *pho*, and it's a very popular breakfast dish in Vietnam, even on hot days.

3. a. It travels from Doha, Qatar, to Auckland, New Zealand.

4. c. The Burj Khalifa has 163 floors and is 2,717 feet tall.

5. c. Australia is in the Southern Hemisphere, so the seasons are opposite! That means Christmas is celebrated during the summer.

6. a. The sun sets for only two hours during the summer solstice because Fairbanks is so far north.

7. b. The Galapagos Islands, near Ecuador, are home of the giant tortoise, which can live to be 100, and Galapagos penguins, which are the only penguins that live north of the Equator.

8. a. In South America, the weather is colder as you head south, away from the Equator.

9. a. Shoes aren't worn inside as a sign of respect and to keep the floors clean. But it's OK to wear slippers inside.

10. c. The Nile River cuts through eleven countries in Africa and is more than 4,000 miles long.

GETTING AROUND

Whether you're riding a train, light-rail, tram, or bus, every city's public transportation has its own personality and is part of the fun of traveling.

Skinkansen
Tokyo, Japan

Tuk tuk
Bangkok, Thailand

Double-decker bus
London, England

Bicycle
Copenhagen, Denmark

DUBLIN
24 JUL 17
IRELAND

Gondola
Venice, Italy

Cable car
San Francisco, USA

where are you going?

When you're in an unfamiliar place, you need to learn how to get around. Luckily, certain rules are the same all over the world.

How to read a map

The first step in knowing where you are going is figuring out where you are! The north, south, east, and west directions of a compass rose will help you. If you step forward, which way are you going? What if you step backward? How about if you turn left? Now right?

Instead of an exact address, sometimes an intersection of two streets can be more helpful. For example, looking at this map, you could say, "The hotel is on Second and Main." If you need to get from the hotel to the bus station, how would you get there? You could travel two blocks north and then one block east. Easy, right?

SugarTown
DOWNTOWN MAP

CHERRY ST

5TH ST

4TH ST

ELM RD

WILLOW ST

AIRPORT

3RD ST

MAIN ST

2ND ST

1ST ST

Travel Tip:

You only need to know one direction of the compass rose to figure out the rest. Think "Never Eat Soggy Waffles" as you take a quarter turn to the right. North, East, South, West!

using public transportation

When you walk into a train station or up to a bus stop, you'll see a map with a lot of lines—and it might seem really confusing. But if you ask yourself these questions, you'll get where you need to go in no time.

1. Where am I?

Where you are determines where you can go. Find where you are on the map. Do you see which colored or numbered line you are near? The lines, or routes, of most trains are colored, and the lines, or routes, for most buses are numbered.

2. Where do I need to go?

Look at the stops along that colored or numbered line. Does the route take you near where you need to go? If yes, great! If no, you may need to take this line to a transfer point and then switch to another line.

A transfer means you'll ride one bus or train line for a few stops, then get off and hop on another bus or train line for a few more stops. Many transportation lines connect like a spider web so you can get to where you need to go—it just might take a bit of time and planning!

3. Figure out which way you need to go.

Each train and bus line will have two options: one line going one way and one line going the opposite way. Each option will have a name, which is usually the last stop on the line. This is how you know which direction the train or bus is heading.

Let's say you get on the subway at the Cherry Street station and you want to go to the Riverwalk Park stop. Which way will you go? You'll take the purple line two stops toward the airport.

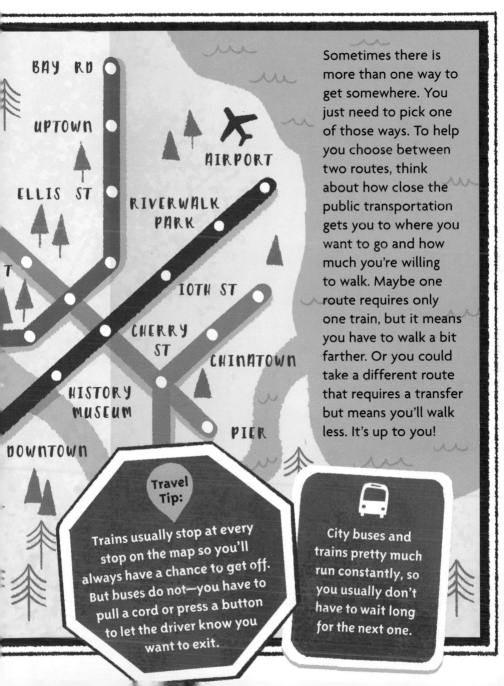

BAY RD

UPTOWN

AIRPORT

ELLIS ST

RIVERWALK PARK

T

10TH ST

CHERRY ST

CHINATOWN

HISTORY MUSEUM

PIER

DOWNTOWN

Sometimes there is more than one way to get somewhere. You just need to pick one of those ways. To help you choose between two routes, think about how close the public transportation gets you to where you want to go and how much you're willing to walk. Maybe one route requires only one train, but it means you have to walk a bit farther. Or you could take a different route that requires a transfer but means you'll walk less. It's up to you!

Travel Tip:

Trains usually stop at every stop on the map so you'll always have a chance to get off. But buses do not—you have to pull a cord or press a button to let the driver know you want to exit.

City buses and trains pretty much run constantly, so you usually don't have to wait long for the next one.

be safe and savvy

These tips and tricks can keep you happy and safe while you're traveling through big cities, bustling crowds, and busy places.

Staying healthy

Wash your hands more than usual when you're traveling. It's easy to pass along illnesses on airplanes, on public transportation, and in other public places.

Don't assume it's OK to drink tap water or even brush your teeth with it if you're in another country. Use bottled water instead. It's never OK to drink water directly from the faucet on an airplane or train.

When you're traveling in another country, think twice before eating from a street cart or food truck. Food should always be fresh, washed with clean water, and cooked thoroughly in a clean kitchen.

Be street smart

When traveling, it's important to be aware of your surroundings, your belongings, and your safety. Tourists can be targets for pickpockets—thieves who secretly steal items from pockets or bags in a crowded area. They are so sneaky that you might not even notice that it happened! These talented thieves know that tourists often carry a lot of cash or expensive cameras and that tourists are often distracted as they try to figure out where they are going in an unfamiliar place.

- On public transportation and at crowded tourist attractions, keep your belongings close to you and your bag zipped. A messenger bag or tote bag with a closed top (a zipper or a flap with a buckle) is the best kind of bag to travel with. Don't put anything in your pockets.

- Don't carry a hotel key card in the envelope the hotel gives you (it says the name of the hotel and your room number, which is unsafe if you lose it). Instead, carry the key and a card with the hotel's name, address, and phone number separately.

- Never count your money in a crowded place. Keep it tucked safely into a zippered wallet or change purse that's kept inside a zippered bag.

Each day, pick a family meeting spot in case anyone gets separated. Cell phones may not work in crowded places, in other countries, or when you're underground on a subway. If you are lost, an adult who works behind a store counter or any uniformed officer (like a police officer or firefighter) can help you.

Travel Tip: Never leave luggage or bags unattended anywhere. Always place your bag in front of you, even when you drink from a water fountain or are waiting in line.

what's your travel style?

Traveling takes skill—you have to find a balance between following a strict schedule and just exploring. See what kind of traveler you are.

1. When you spend the night at a friend's house, you are worried . . .

   a. things might be different from what you're used to.

   b. about nothing! Your friend will plan fun stuff to do.

   c. that you'll be bored and not have enough to do.

2. Your birthday party is in a few weeks. You . . .

   a. have had every detail planned for weeks.

   b. still haven't sent out the invitations.

   c. can't decide on a theme. You have too many good ideas!

3. Your friends want to watch a movie. You'd like to watch one that . . .

   a. all your friends have seen before and love.

   b. no one has seen before.

   c. at least two friends promise is good.

4. For lunch at school, you always . . .

   a. bring your own.

   b. eat whatever the special is that day.

   c. order the same thing.

5. You have to give a speech today. You'll be fine as long as you have . . .

   a. your lucky key chain. It always helps!

   b. courage! You know you can do this.

   c. hours and hours of practice.

6. On a long road trip, you bring along a . . .

   a. favorite book to pass the time.

   b. brand-new game you want to try.

   c. few books and games so you have options.

Olive leaf

MENU

7. You get to pick a dinner spot for your birthday. You . . .

   a. pick the same restaurant you go to every year.

   b. tell your family to surprise you.

   c. have a hard time deciding between three different places.

Answers

If you picked **mostly a's,** you're a planner. You feel most comfortable when you're in control. You like to pick out what you're going to do, eat, and see because it's fun, and you know you'll enjoy yourself. Remember, though, just because something is unfamiliar to you— or is not your own idea—doesn't mean that it's bad. Step outside your comfort zone and let someone else take the wheel for a bit. Travel is a great time to practice this skill.

If you picked **mostly b's,** you like to wing it! You're open to trying new things, and you're perfectly fine going with the flow. You're easy-going, which means you don't need to plan much. This quality makes you a great traveler, but know that it's OK to voice your opinion sometimes. When you totally wing it, you may miss out on some experiences that you would have loved. A little planning ahead can help with this. Your opinions matter!

If you picked **mostly c's,** you're a wanderer. You love to research and explore. You're con-stantly looking for the next cool thing and gathering plenty of options. Sometimes you have so many options that you have a hard time making a decision. Accept that you'll never be able to do and see everything, and instead fully enjoy the experiences you have. When you travel, try prioritizing each day with the three most important activities. That way you'll still have time to explore, but you'll be sure to see the things that excite you the most.

63

TRYING NEW THINGS

It's time to be brave and step outside your comfort zone. Replace fear of the unknown with excitement!

But I've never tried that before.

Maybe I'll like it.

It looks weird.

It looks interesting.

I don't think I'll like that.

It's worth a try.

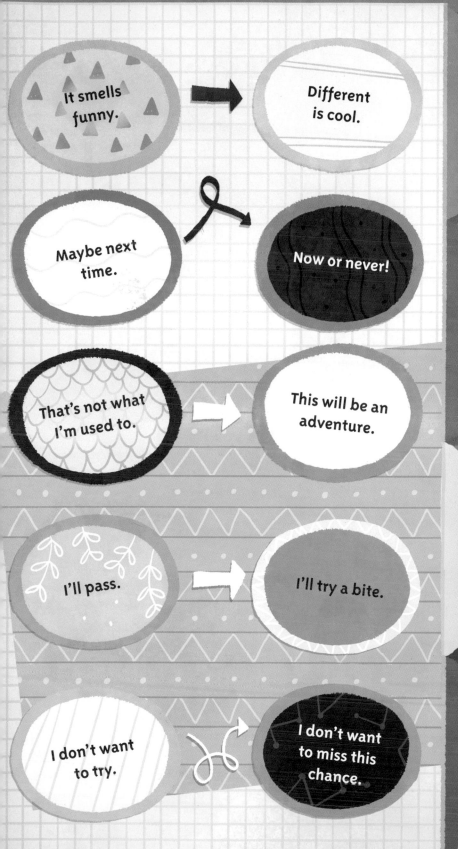

65

eye spy

It's time to be a super sleuth! There's so much to take in when you visit a new place. Whether you're visiting a different part of your hometown or another side of the world, you are sure to spot a lot of differences. Document your findings with a camera or write them down in a travel journal.

Street Signs

Are they a different shape, color, or design?

Music

What are people listening to? Do you recognize it?

Food

What are people eating for breakfast, lunch, and dinner?

Dessert

What sweet treats do you see?

Clothing

How does everyone dress? What do their shoes and bags look like?

Homes

Where do people live? How is it different from your home?

Hairstyles

Have you ever worn your hair like that?

Language

Do they speak another language or use slang that's new to you?

Schools

Do kids wear uniforms? How do they get to school? What do the schools look like?

Pets

What kind of pets do you see walking around?

JELLY

Grocery Stores

What kind of candy, drinks, and snacks are they selling?

Transportation

Which side of the road are the cars driving on? Are people riding bikes or buses?

global grub

These are some of the most popular dishes in countries around the world. Which one do you want to try?

If you like mac and cheese, try . . . **palak paneer (India)**.

Soft cheese cubes cooked in a spinach curry sauce.

If you like chicken noodle soup, try . . . **ramen (Japan)**.

A noodle soup often topped with sliced pork and a soft-boiled egg.

If you like chicken fingers, try . . . **falafel (Israel)**.

Fried chickpea balls that can be eaten alone or served in a pita bread pocket.

If you like sushi rolls, try . . . **ceviche (Peru)**.

Fresh raw fish that's topped with lemon or lime juice.

If you like pizza, try . . . **meat pie (Australia)**.

A small, savory meat-filled pie served warm with tomato sauce.

Sweet stuff

Desserts may look different, but people around the world have one thing in common: a sweet tooth!

If you like pancakes, try . . . crepes (France).

A thin pancake spread with sweets such as chocolate hazelnut spread, bananas, and powdered sugar, and then folded into a triangle.

If you like ice cream, try . . . gelato (Italy).

A softer, thicker, smoother version of ice cream. Try fruit flavors such as lemon and peach or creamy flavors like chocolate or hazelnut.

If you like toaster pastries, try . . . apfelstrudel (Austria).

A flaky pastry with warm apple filling inside.

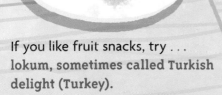

If you like fruit snacks, try . . . lokum, sometimes called Turkish delight (Turkey).

Colorful and chewy gel-like cubes with nuts inside. Common flavors are rose water and orange.

If you like caramel, try . . . dulce de leche (Argentina).

Milk and sugar are heated until a caramel-like sauce is formed.

languages around the world

There are about 7,000 languages spoken around the world! But don't worry—you don't need to learn them all. A majority of the world speaks only a handful of these languages. The most popular language is Mandarin Chinese, followed by Spanish, English, Hindi, and Arabic. If you know one—or more—of these five languages, it may be a little easier for you to communicate when you travel around the world.

Mandarin Chinese

Hello: Ni hao
(nee-how)

你好

Good-bye: Zai jian
(dzye yan)

再见

Please: Qing
(ching)

请

Thank you: Xiexie ni
(shyeh-shyeh nee)

谢谢

Spanish

Hello: Hola
(OH-la)

Please: Por favor
(por fah-VOR)

Good-bye: Adiós
(ah-dee-OHS)

Thank you: Gracias
(GRAH-see-ahs)

Hindi

Hello: Namaste
(nuhm-uh-stay)

नमस्ते

Good-bye: Namaste
(nuhm-uh-stay)

नमस्ते

Please: Kripya
(kri-pa-yaa)

कृप्या

Thank you: Shukriyaa
(shuk-ri yah)

शुक्रिया

Arabic

Hello: Al-salāmu 'alaykum
(as-salaam alaykum)

السَّلامُ عَلَيْكُم

Good-bye: Ma' al salāmah
(ma as-salaama)

مَع السَّلامة

Please: Min fadlak
(min faDlak)

من فضلك

Thank you: Shukran
(shoo-kran)

شكرا

Where in the World?

Here are the most common places you'll find these languages spoken.

Mandarin Chinese: China and Singapore

Spanish: Europe, Central America, and South America

English: United States, Canada, United Kingdom, Australia, and New Zealand

Hindi: India and Nepal

Arabic: North Africa and the Middle East

BACK AT HOME

Part of the fun of travel is dreaming up where you can go one day and reminiscing about where you've already been. And you can do all that from your couch!

armchair travel

You don't have to leave your hometown—or even your home—to embark on a new adventure. There are plenty of ways to learn about the world, and many of them are free!

Learn a new language. Pick up a book or language DVD at the library, or sign up for a class.

Read a fiction book about a place you'd love to visit. Imagine what it would be like to go there in real life.

Go for a walk or hike with your family in a park you've never visited. Navigate your way there using a map.

Explore a local museum. The art and artifacts inside traveled from all over the world to your town.

Watch a travel show about a place you've never been. Is it a place you'd like to visit one day?

Do you live near a big city? It may have a neighborhood like Little India or Chinatown. Explore the restaurants and shops.

Spin a globe, let your finger fall on a random place, and then ask a parent to research it with you online.

Check out a travel guidebook from the library, and then create a weeklong itinerary for a faraway place.

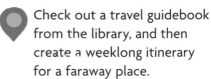

Visit a restaurant that serves food from a country you'd like to visit. Write a review afterward and share it with your friends.

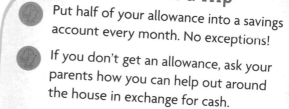

Draw a map of your neighborhood or hometown. Include all the important places you think a visitor would like to see.

ISLE OF ROSE

How to Save for a Trip

Put half of your allowance into a savings account every month. No exceptions!

If you don't get an allowance, ask your parents how you can help out around the house in exchange for cash.

Start a business. Offer to babysit, rake leaves, or walk the dog for your neighbors.

Every little bit counts. Temporarily cut back on treats and trinkets and instead make an effort to save for something big.

Sell your old toys, games, clothes, and stuffed animals at a garage sale or an online marketplace—with an adult's permission of course!

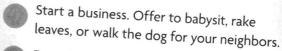
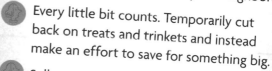

making and keeping memories

The best thing you'll collect during your travels are the memories—they're free and don't take up any room in your suitcase. Here are some ways to help you remember all the awesome sights and cool experiences.

- Keep a travel journal and write in it each night during your trip. Write down where you went, how you got there, what you saw, what you ate, and any interesting or funny things that happened.

- Mail yourself a postcard at the end of your trip. Sum up all the highlights. It will be a nice surprise once you get home. (Send one to a friend, too!)

Hello from Switzerland! It's beautiful here, there are so many tall mountains!

Jenni Ota
2 Pine Rd
SF, CA

- Start a family blog and take turns sharing updates and photos from your adventures each day. It will be fun to go back and read these posts later.

Travel Tip: Make sure to get plenty of photos with you and your family in them—instead of just photos of buildings, vistas, or landmarks. It can also be fun to take pics of the food you ate, the cool street signs you saw, and the transportation you took.

- Bring along a camera and capture images each day. When you get home, put your photos in an album online or print them and make a scrapbook.

What makes a good souvenir?

You may be tempted to bring home something besides photos and memories. But souvenirs are often expensive, and they can take up a lot of room in your suitcase. Instead, start a simple collection of small items that you can add to each time you travel. Here are some ideas:

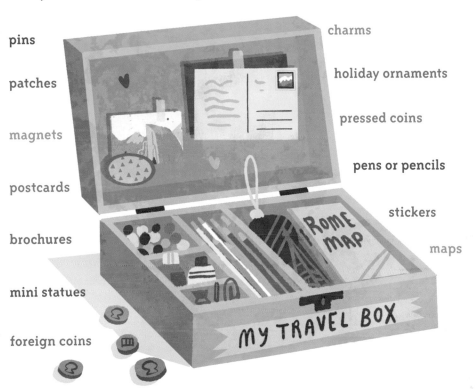

pins

patches

magnets

postcards

brochures

mini statues

foreign coins

charms

holiday ornaments

pressed coins

pens or pencils

stickers

maps

If you want to some-thing special to help com-memorate your travels, spend your money on a one-of-a-kind item that you could never find at home—and make sure it's some-thing you'll actually use. A handmade tote bag from a small shop can be used to carry books to school in style. Unique candy from a corner grocery store will come in handy on a long plane ride and can be fun to share with friends back at home.

WANDERLUST

It's that feeling when you want to get out and explore, a longing to pack your bags and travel someplace new, or a sudden urge for adventure.

exciting cities

Visiting a foreign city is like meeting a new friend. Each one has its own quirks, flavors, and curiosities.

London, England

This British city is full of iconic sights, such as Buckingham Palace, where the Queen of England lives, and the London Eye, a giant Ferris wheel. Be sure to see a play or musical in the West End—London is where many of Shakespeare's plays were first performed.

Dubai, United Arab Emirates

Dubai is home to the tallest building in the world, the Burj Khalifa. It's more than 160 stories high! Even though this city is located in the Arabian Desert, there's an indoor ski hill where it's actually cold and snowy.

Toronto, Canada

Toronto is the biggest city in Canada and is said to be the most diverse city on the planet. More than 140 languages are spoken here. Most signs are written in English and French—that's because the country is bilingual and has two official languages.

Venice, Italy

In this city, there are no roads for cars. That means you'll walk a lot! As you stroll through narrow alleys and over the bridges of the many canals, you'll get a close-up look at the marble palaces that appear to magically float on the lagoon. When your feet need a break, hop in a gondola or a water taxi.

Rio de Janeiro, Brazil

This seaside city has lush mountains and beautiful beaches, such as Copacabana and Ipanema. It's also known for Carnaval—the world's largest festival that ends with a huge samba dance-off. Here's a fun fact: Brazil is the only country in South America where people speak Portuguese, not Spanish.

Istanbul, Turkey

Istanbul is located on two different continents—part of the city is in Europe and part is in Asia. A waterway called the Bosporus Strait divides the city, but bridges make it easy to walk from one side to the other. Visitors love stepping inside the colorful mosques and shopping in the bustling bazaars, or marketplaces.

iconic sights

Seeing these incredible structures in person reminds you of the many people who came before you and all the interesting cultures that make the world such a diverse and fascinating place.

Great Pyramids of Giza, 2700–2500 BCE

These three Egyptian pyramids are incredibly old. The largest one held the title of tallest structure in the world for almost 4,000 years. No one knows for sure how these royal tombs were built without modern tools.

Colosseum, 70 CE

In this Roman amphitheater, or sports arena, gladiators used to fight each other as 50,000 people cheered them on. Now visitors walk inside the ruins and imagine the ancient spectacles.

Angkor Wat, 9th to 15th Centuries

Adventurers love to tour the jungle ruins of Angkor Wat in Siem Reap, Cambodia. Trees grow and monkeys scamper among these ancient remains. Watching sunrise at the main temple is number one on many travelers' must-see lists.

Machu Picchu, 15th to 16th Centuries

These ancient Incan ruins can be found high up in the Andes Mountains in Peru, and only a certain number of visitors are allowed each year in order to protect them. Today, people take a train ride or a multi-day hike just to get a glimpse.

The Great Wall, 14th to 17th Centuries

The Great Wall of China extends about 13,000 miles. Every year, millions of visitors walk along the wall, which was originally built to keep invading armies out.

Eiffel Tower, 1889

When this 1,000-foot tower was built for the World's Fair, it was the tallest structure at the time. Now it's the most popular paid tourist attraction on the planet. Visitors can ride an elevator to the top for a bird's-eye view of Paris.

Famous artwork

Imagine seeing one of these masterpieces in person.

Mona Lisa
by Leonardo da Vinci
The Louvre, Paris

Las Dos Fridas by Frida Kahlo
Museo de Arte Moderno,
Mexico City

Black Iris
by Georgia O'Keeffe
The Metropolitan
Museum of Art,
New York City

A Sunday on La Grande Jatte
by Georges Seurat
Art Institute of Chicago

The Starry Night
by Vincent van Gogh
Museum of Modern Art,
New York City

natural wonders

Our Earth is a breathtaking, fascinating, and inspiring place. Cities are cool, but nature is even more impressive. You can plan entire trips around some amazing sights.

Angel Falls

At more than 3,000 feet, Venezuela's Angel Falls is the tallest waterfall in the world. Because of its remote location, it's an adventure just to get there—via plane, then a boat, then a hiking trail.

Ha Long Bay

This magical bay in Vietnam is dotted with more than 1,000 tiny jungle islands. The best way to experience Ha Long Bay is to drift by the cliffs on a boat and just take in the beautiful views.

The Grand Canyon

It sure is grand—it's eighteen miles wide and about a mile deep! Every year, more than five million people travel to Arizona to take in the canyon's natural beauty. Sunset and sunrise are especially colorful, and some people hike all the way down into the canyon to camp.

Galapagos Islands

This isolated chain of volcanic islands off the coast of Ecuador is known for incredible wildlife—some of which can only be found here. Small cruise ships ferry travelers around to see giant turtles, penguins, albatross, and more. Naturalist Charles Darwin studied here when he was developing his theory of evolution.

Mauna Kea

On the Big Island of Hawaii lies a sacred dormant volcano that rises almost 14,000 feet above the sea. It's a favorite site for astronomers and amateur stargazers because it is one of the clearest places in the world to view the night sky. This may be Hawaii, but make sure you bundle up before a visit— it often snows at the top!

The Dead Sea

Found between Jordan and Israel, the Dead Sea is incredibly unique. It's the lowest place on Earth, and it's extra salty—ten times saltier than any ocean. Travelers who wade into this turquoise lake quickly learn how easy it is to float. Visitors also like to slather their skin with Dead Sea mud, which is full of minerals. **85**

hooray for the USA

The United States is big. If you flew from Miami to Seattle, it would take almost seven hours. Each corner of the country is so unique, with different accents, food, weather, sights, and more.

The East Coast

This is the part of the country where you'll find fresh seafood and big cities along the Atlantic Ocean.

Learn about immigration . . . The Statue of Liberty has been greeting visitors to the United States since 1886. From 1892 to 1954, many people who immigrated, or moved to the United States from another country, arrived at nearby Ellis Island. To visit the statue's crown, you must climb 393 steps—there's no elevator inside the statue!

Feel patriotic . . . In Washington, D.C., you can tour the nation's capitol building and get a pic in front of the White House. Many of the museums in D.C. are free and are filled with historic artifacts such as the Declaration of Independence and Abraham Lincoln's top hat.

The South

People say life is a little more laid-back in the South and that the people are friendly—maybe it's because the weather is warmer!

Experience one-of-a-kind culture . . .
New Orleans is home to two unique cultures: Cajun and Creole. Did you know many people used to speak French here? The city is also known for delicious food like gumbo and jambalaya as well as being the birthplace of jazz music.

The Midwest

The middle of the country is known for being friendly. Many of the cities here popped up along the shores of the Great Lakes, which is a chain of five huge lakes: Huron, Ontario, Michigan, Erie, and Superior.

Look up to the sky . . .
In Chicago, skyscrapers line the shores of Lake Michigan and the Chicago River—four of the ten tallest buildings in the United States are here. From the top of the Willis Tower, you can see four states: Wisconsin, Illinois, Indiana, and Michigan.

The Southwest

You can easily travel from the mountains to the desert in this part of the country, which is known for its Native American influences.

Take in the mountain views . . .
Towns in Colorado such as Vail, Aspen, and Breckenridge were built among the mountains and are perfect destinations for skiing and snowboarding. The state gets fresh snow all winter long, sometimes as early as October and as late as April.

Step back in time . . .
Santa Fe, New Mexico, is the country's oldest capital city—and the highest. It's known for its historic Pueblo-style architecture. The buildings' soft curves and brown color blend in with nature because the bricks are made from mud.

The Northwest

This is where the mountains meet the ocean, which makes the Pacific Northwest an especially beautiful place to visit—and eat fresh seafood.

See animals in the wild . . .
Forget the zoo! Visit Alaska and you're sure to see amazing wildlife —bears, moose, whales, seals, and more, in their natural habitat. Alaska is a beautiful mix of mountains, forest, and ocean that's unlike any other state in the country.

The West Coast

This was one of the last parts of the United States to be settled and it's known for its contrast of sparkling ocean views and harsh desert life.

Bike across a landmark . . .
When San Francisco's Golden Gate Bridge was built in 1937, it was the longest and tallest suspension bridge at the time. Now it's said to be the most photographed bridge in the world. It's fun for visitors to walk, bike, or drive across the huge bridge.

what's your dream trip?

Some trips are extra special. They may be extra far away, take an extra long time to save up for, or just make you feel extra excited. See which dream trip is perfect for you.

1. You would love to spend an afternoon . . .

   a. cuddling with your pet.

   b. riding your bike.

   c. watching your favorite movie.

   d. relaxing outside.

2. You're not afraid to . . .

   a. live without TV and Internet for a week.

   b. sleep outside under the stars.

   c. try to learn another language.

   d. go snorkeling in the ocean.

3. If you could visit only one place, you would pick . . .

   a. a jungle.

   b. the mountains.

   c. a city.

   d. a beach.

4. When you travel, you want to . . .

   a. see something unusual.

   b. try something exciting.

   c. experience a different culture.

   d. take in beautiful sights.

5. Your friends say that you're . . .

   a. sweet and caring.

   b. daring and fun.

   c. curious and interesting.

   d. easygoing and chill.

6. On a trip, it would be nice if . . .

   a. someone else planned every day for me.

   b. you were in charge of where you'd go each day.

   c. you could wander around on your own time.

   d. you could just relax and not worry about anything.

7. One day, you'd love to work in a job that supports . . .

   a. animal rights.

   b. being fit and healthy.

   c. arts and music.

   d. oceans and lakes.

Answers

If you picked **mostly a's,** you're an animal lover, and an African safari is perfect for you. Imagine sleeping in a tent but knowing that a lion might walk by while you're snoozing! When you're on an African safari, a guide will drive you around in hopes of spotting the big five in the wild: lion, leopard, elephant, rhinoceros, and buffalo. Kenya's Masai Mara National Reserve and Tanzania's Serengeti National Park are popular places to go on safari.

If you picked **mostly b's,** you're an adventure seeker, and you'd love Yellowstone National Park for hiking, biking, horseback riding, camping, rafting, ziplining, and more. As an adventure lover, you'll never get bored at Yellowstone. In addition to all the outdoor activities, there's a lot to see. Mostly located in Wyoming, the park is filled with unbelievable sights such as waterfalls, geysers, and hot springs. People travel from all over the world to experience nature like this.

If you picked **mostly c's,** you're totally into culture and you'd love Japan for the fashion, technology, food, music, and more. You'll feel as if you've stepped back in time as you walk through temples in Kyoto, and you'll feel as if you've traveled to the future when you walk the busy streets of Tokyo. Good thing the trains in Japan are super fast so you can see a lot in one trip.

If you picked **mostly d's,** you're a beach lover, and a trip to Australia is perfect for you. Flights to Australia are long—it takes about seventeen hours to fly from Houston, Texas, to Sydney. But once you get there, you'll instantly relax thanks to the laid-back vibe. You'll love watching surfers splash in the waves while you soak up the sun on Bondi Beach. And you won't want to miss the Great Barrier Reef in Queensland. It's the largest collection of coral reefs in the world.

You can be a traveler

You don't have to go far to start exploring or to lead a life full of adventure. What are you waiting for? Get out there!

Be open to learning new things.

Ask questions.

Make observations.

Walk around in another country using Google Maps Street View.

Talk to people who are different from you.

Do you have a travel tale to tell?

Write to us!
Travel Editor
American Girl
8400 Fairway Place
Middleton, WI 53562

Here are some other American Girl books you might like:

Each sold separately. Find more books online at americangirl.com.